SONGS FOR MY HAIR

Lyrics of Love, Life, Loss, and Surviving Breast Cancer

by

CHE'VONCEIL ECHOLS, PhD

Copyright 2017 Che'Vonceil Echols, PhD

All rights reserved

TABLE OF CONTENTS

Dedication vi
Forward vii
From Pain to Power... vii

SONGS OF LOVE
I

A Song For My Hair 2
I Am Colored Pecola 10
Hold Me While I Cry 14
Will He Still Love Me Tomorrow?..15
Just Let Me Be Something 22
The Morning Is So Beautiful...24
I'm Still Here…Still Waiting 26
Look At Me! 32
Me and My Fender Rhodes 34
Your Smile Throws Me...37
When I Look at Your Face 38
My Greatest Love 40
I Will Come Home Again 42
Vessel of Love 44
My Dance 47

I Remember Mama 50
I Am a Thread 56
My Bed 63

SONGS OF LIFE
II

Freedom is Coming Today! 66
My Tribute Part I 68
My Tribute Part II 72
My Tribute Part III 76
I SO LA TION 79
Who Am I 80
Testing, Testing…1…2…3…Testing! 82
The Weary Round of Life 88
I'm Crossing Over 89
On Wings 91
I Can't Believe This Man! 93
Inside the House That Crack Built 95
Being Beautiful is a Suffering Way 97
My Journey 99
Survivors Dissertation/ The Year of Jubilee 101
Inside My Skin #1 106
I am the one 108
What If 116

SONGS OF LOSS
III

If I Should Die…I Love 119
Our Diamond Dove 123
I Don't Want to Die 126
Goodnight, Granny Echols 128
Ghost 130
The Bear 131

IT..133
The Secret..134

SONG OF SURVIVAL
IV

You Are Not Forgotten 137
About the Author 141
Bibliography 143

Dedication

This Book is dedicated to my beloved parents
Walter Montgomery and Vonceil Evelyn Echols, and
my beloved children, Lee, Angela, and Jaden Hairston.
It is dedicated to all those who have played an
inspirational part in the creation
of *Songs for My Hair:*
Love, Life, Loss, and Surviving Breast Cancer.
Your names may not be written on this page
but they are written in my heart
and on every line of every poem.
I thank you.

Che'Vonceil Echols, Ph.D.

Forward

From Pain to Power

Have you ever found yourself in God's spiritual solitude and confinement camp, where the most difficult, painful, and, for sure, lonely of times seem to never end?
Have you ever battled shame and personal embarrassment?
Have you fought back resentment, anger, and jealousy?
Have you ever struggled with doubt and disbelief and had a lack of confidence?
Have you ever stopped feeling, caring, and crying?
Have you ever wanted to die?
Or lost your joy, your anointing, and your testimony?
Have you ever wanted to run away from the pain, the hurt, because the feelings of betrayal ran so deep? Did you ever think that you would never love again? Feel again or believe again?
Have you ever been wounded in the house of God?
You managed somehow to hold on. You managed to keep at bay the runaway spirit. You managed to fast. You kept on praising God and pressed on when you wanted to give up. You knew that God had a purpose for this pain.
The Lord wanted you to take a long, hard look at yourself.
You had to acknowledge your sense of pride, your most holy arrogance, and your presumptuousness. You thought you were God's golden child. You could do no wrong.

You thought that you were so special that God would even overlook your sins!
Your carelessness with his holiness!
Everything you had was slowly being taken away from you.
It was the beginning of the ability to break away.

You were removed from all that had esteemed you highly!
The power and influence of leadership.
The private office where you ministered to those who needed you!
Not God but you!
You had the keys to the Holy Mansion, the keys to the Holy Cabinets, and the keys to the Holy Pastor's office.
The secret combination to get in and out of the Holy Mansion!

You were a great somebody.
You had a private parking spot and a special Sunday morning seat. A charter member with all rights and privileges!
But you stank in the face of God Almighty
and were dust under His fingernails.
What was so amazing?
You kept singing, praising, and testifying to how great God is but thinking, 'How great I AM!'
God had revealed to you that He had a greater purpose for your life than just your loving yourself!
But you didn't listen.
You went on your way in all your splendor and glory.
You prayed, "Lord use me,
break me and make me over again!"

As soon as those words came out of your mouth,
you began to wrestle against the will
of God.
Be careful what you pray for!
It was your time to be weighed in the balance. It was your time to be measured. It was your time to be shaken, proven to see if you were truly for God or against his purposes.
At first you wanted to blame everybody for what was happening to you. Your keys were being taken from you one by one!
You weren't president, coordinator, supervisor, counselor, poet, praise leader, lead singer, organizer, Sunday school teacher, Bible scholar, or confidant to the pastor
anymore!
You began to search your own inconsistencies and consider your own negative behavior. You could hold only yourself accountable for your own doings. You continued going to the house, you continued to praise God, you continued to give and to testify. Your desire was for the Holy Ghost to reign supreme in the face of adversity.
You prayed for a new thing to happen in your life. You didn't need to be president to serve. You didn't need to be chairperson to lead. You didn't need to be the soloist to sing. You didn't need to have an office to counsel. You didn't need to have the keys to be a good example or to be respected.

That woman I speak of is me…

It was at a women's retreat where I placed my prayer

request into a burning campfire. I had suggested that all of the women give a request to the Lord and send it up as a sweet-smelling savor.

In my lack of wisdom and my presumptuousness, I placed the prayer that changed my life into the fire.

I prayed...

"Lord, break me and make me over again."

I knew in fantasy what I was asking for but not in reality what I would get!

The Lord put me in a place of solitude. I was in the ranks of leadership one day and then a part of the laity the next. I had been saved for 25 years at the time. I was always in the role of a leader and a member of the pastoral family.

All of the works I had rendered were replaced by the works that I had to do in the body now. I was always in a certain place, doing certain things, receiving certain praises, respected by certain people who only accepted me in those certain situations. Now that I was not holding those certain positions, they treated me a certain way!

I learned that change is one of the most difficult things to go through. It was a changing of the guard, going out of the office, not being a part of the "inner circle." It feels like you are a misfit in the house of God. You're not in the leadership ranks anymore but you feel out of sorts in the laity ranks.

I don't think that was God's plan.

Are we not all workers for the body of Christ?

The Lord began to break up the fallow ground within me. Some folks think that if you are in church leadership, you are always prayed up, fasted up, and read up, that the anointing is always flowing in your life. I think that the most difficult place to be is in the pot-shot of Christian critics.

Your most holy work takes the biggest toll on your life. It is an all-consuming job. Folks feel that if you work for God full-time, you are supposed to be available all of the time.
They don't realize that thinking like that is a sure-fire ticket to the
Bahamas burnout festival!

I dreamed a destiny.
I had a series of dreams that revealed that I would be stepping out in faith in a new vineyard. That I should not fear. That He would grant me favor, a covering, and friendship like I had never experienced before. That the purpose for which He had called me would unfold:
"Line upon line and precept upon precept."
That it was time to move from pain to power.
The lessons that I had learned, the foundation that I had received, were also a part of God's plan for my life.
Have I done all things well?
No!
Have I made mistakes?
Yes!
Do I have regrets?
Yes.

I have broken ground so that God can build again.
I have stepped out of the box,
come from behind the wall,
and
I am moving
from pain to power,
from promise to purpose!

This book of poetic prose has taken a lifetime to write.
I have been bound by fear and procrastination.
Today I am allowing myself to step out into my destiny.
I am a prophetic poet!
I have never said those words before. I know that God has called me into the ministry of words.
Like King David,
I am a poet!

I

SONGS OF LOVE

A love song for Sherri DyAnne

A Song For My Hair

Every time I brushed her hair, I filled my pockets with despair
Afraid to let her see the fear inside of me
She cried,
"I want to go back inside my mother's safe, warm womb
I want to cry there,
Lie there, sometimes I wish that I had died there…
Because inside my mother's womb I don't need no hair
I don't even care about hair!"
Some say a woman's hair is her glory but that's not her story.
And when it was all gone, she questioned…
Does that mean that I am no longer glorious?
No longer favored?
No longer beautiful?
No longer desirous?
No longer wanting?
No longer sensuous?
Will other women
See me but not want to be me?
When my glory is gone…
When my glory is all gone.
My hair is almost gone now. I am not bald but my hair is well…
"Scarce as hens' teeth!"
I am the image of every woman's dreaded nightmare.
I can't throw my hair back and feel the ebb and flow of

my locks embracing my shoulders or touching my face anymore!
I can't brush it every night with one hundred long, loving, luscious, liquid strokes, waiting for it to grow!
I can't curl it around my fingers or fashion it into a stunning style that *he* admires and *she* envies!
I can't twist it into a thousand tiny braids embraced with shells from the Congo coast or celebrate or even boast of my ethnicity!
I can't color it, perm it, relax it, oil it, style it, cut it, grow it and you know it!
It has lost its shine, gleam, glow, Breck hair flow and wouldn't you know...
It has lost its curl and beaded twists
It won't knot and oh! I almost forgot
Hold neither clips, flowers, or rhinestones; hairpins not needed here!
It's my hair and I'll cry if I want to; you would too if this happened to you.
The Cancer has succeeded. My hairline has receded!
It's not nappy, silky, straight, shaggy, or matted.
It is just not brilliant anymore.
It won't tangle, mangle, or dangle!
Because I'm bald, the Cancer!
The gall of it all
Want to know what her *dream* is?
She whispered...
My hair is but a slither now but in my dreams...in my dreams...
My hair extends all the way across the seven continents and winds its way back
To my mother's womb where hair doesn't matter

Che'Vonceil Echols, PhD

My hair is like the satin Black Panther cat from Dakar,
My hair has ferocious vigor and form
It is unique, not like the norm.
My hair carries the torch of the world's symbol of beauty
and as it dies
I claim *my* voice and pronounce my will to live!
My hair stretches out into a bridge
Cradling baby hair from birth to rebirth.
My hair makes me want to scrape my knees in prayer and
Lord!
A wig is something I just don't dig!
That's my dream but this is my *reality*
I cannot attach any hair extensions to my bald scalp
Or glue hair in or sew it on.
I polish my head instead
And stopped wishing that I were dead!
You heard what I said!
It's my hair and I can cry if I want to; you would too if
this happened to you!
It doesn't matter what my race is
Or what color my face is
Cancer! There, I've said it again!
It doesn't hear my cry or see my pain!
Please hear ME!!!
It doesn't matter what your race is
Or what color your face is
To name a few, you could be
African
Asian
South American
European
Gentile or

Jew
People think that your hair is YOU!
It's about acceptance
And I know that's the truth!
She lifted her voice and sang a song for her hair...
I am no longer ashamed of it!
I have renamed it!
I have reclaimed it!
My HAIR
Glorified it!
Celebrated it!
Emancipated it!
My HAIR
Congratulated it!
Anticipated It!
Applauded it!
My Hair
I'm standing in ovation of it!
I'm praising it!
Shouting about it!
I've learned how to live without it!
My Hair
If you care
Can I get an Amen right there?
My nemesis Cancer...
Her radical Chemo-devastation
Kills from the inside out
It attacks the bloodstream, that's what I'm talking about!
Destroys hair follicles
Turns beauty to ashes
Hopes into molecules...
When it was my turn to cry, I faced the bathroom mirror

Locked the door and
Looked straight into myself. I saw no hair where eyelashes used to be
And I cried,
And I cried,
And I cried,
And I cried
I tried to hide it from them and him
Until I had no hair left
And no left breast…You want to know the rest?
It appalled him, galled him
He turned away when my scarf fell off!
I wore wraps, hats, caps, and crowns
But none embraced me with such disdain as the pity in his eyes.
He knew no better. His love sustains me now.
My scarves a disguise for my scars
And my sunglasses hid the pain inside my eyes
It's my hair and I'll cry if I want to; you would too if this happened to you!
My Hair she sings…
My hair, you make me fairest of them all
You are my crown of glory
Made with gold and silver threads
My hair adorned with stars and galaxies
Asteroids and constellations exploding!
I embrace you now
My Hair
I hold you in my hands
I lift you up to the sapphire sky and my song will carry you out into the universal sea where there are others just like me

My hair is an offering to life
Faith, trust, and hope
My precious strands
A blend of cultures
Black, brown, blond, red,
Auburn and gray
We will all have hair again one day!
In celebration
I've decided to name my hair
I name it in honor of survivors and my sisters who have
Crossed over to the other side.
I Name it Julie Brown King
Who succumbed when the poem was done!
Girl, can you hear me sing?
Because your song is being sung.
I Name it Patricia Hinsley a soul survivor and my dearest friend
For my childhood friend Helen Keys, this is for you, girl
I remember your voice saying, "Write the poem poet please!"
I name it for my niece Alexis Vonceil, at seventeen,
who never got to fulfill her dreams
For my Aunt Dorothy, rest in peace
Four cousins still in the fight!

For my grandma Mattie
Who died one night

I name it for Bodacious Belinda J. Echols-Heard, who says...
"A Fly Diva don't need 'no' hair!"
Hey girls, are you out there?

I name it Queen Marion Moultrie and
Princess Sherri DyAnne
Mademoiselle and Madame
Cancer doesn't care whose country I am!
I name it for my Aunt Grace, for deaf sisters too!
The seeing and the blind, you know what you've gotta do!
This is a song for my sisters who survived!
Cancer thought it was your end but...
Thank God...you're still alive!!

Sherri DyAnne

I Am Colored Pecola

(The name "Pecola" is inspired by Toni Morrison's character in **The Bluest Eye.***)*

I Am Colored Pecola
In My House There Are No Mirrors
I See The Beauty Of Who I Am, Through My Mama's Eyes
My Large Shaped Almond Eyes, Mama Says…
One Is Like The Sun Rising And Setting; Creating Each New Day
The Other Is Like The Moon, Leaving Its Afterglow On Me
I Am Colored Pecola
The Color Of Pain
I Didn't Want No Near-Sighted, Almond-Shaped Brown Eyes!
I Wanted Blue Eyes. Hazel, Gray, Or Even Green
They're Prettier It Seems And Round, Full, And Flirtatious
I'd Be Bodacious!
I Am Colored Pecola
My Mama Said My Lips Were Plump
And Naturally Pink!
She Said When I Smiled My High Cheekbones
Rose Up Like Mountains
She'd Say, "Go Kiss The Day With Your Sweet Morning Dew Smile!"

I Am Colored Pecola
The Color Of Self-Hate And Societies' Shameful Victim
Of Rape!
I Didn't Want No Pink Fat Lips!
I Wanted Two. Thin. Red. Lips!
My Mama Said, "Your Teeth Are Like The White Picket
Fence
I Dreamed Of In Dreams."
My Teeth Were Like Hope
I Am Colored Pecola
The Color Of One Mocked
My Teeth Ain't No White Picket Fence!
I Got Buck Teeth And Braces
I Was The Laughingstock Of The Eighth Grade
No Shade...
Hope Rhymes With Dope!
I Am Colored Pecola
My Mama Said, "You Have Hair Like An African
Queen."
I Said,
"Who, Mama? You Don't Know No African Queens!
Who?"
"Nzinga, The Warrior Queen," She Said...
"With Hair Like Lamb's Wool; Curly, Wild, Kinky,
Nappy, Full Of Static, Electric, Powerful, Glorious, And
Mysterious Hair!"
I Am Colored Pecola
The Color Of Disdain
I Didn't Want No Lamb's Wool, Curly, Wild, Kinky,
Nappy, Full Of Static, Electric, Powerful, Glorious, And
Mysterious Hair!
I Wanted A Press N Curl!

Ain't No Queens Live In Buffalo No How!
I Am Colored Pecola
My Mama Said, "You're Not Fat, Precious, You're Pleasingly Plump!
You Inherited My Hips And Breasts."
Her Breasts 40 Double E! I Was Ashamed. Don't look At Me!
I Am Colored Pecola
I Am A Full-Figured Woman Who Is Always Complimented On How Well I Carry My Weight.
Mama Said, "Look Into My Eyes, Child. You Are Beautiful!
You Are Diamonds, Rubies, Emeralds, And Pearls.
You Are God's Child, In All Of His Magnificence!"
I Am Colored Pecola
I Was Twenty Then, I Didn't Want No Full Figure
I Was Tired Of Carrying My Weight!
I Cried Myself To Sleep For Thirty Years!
When I Finally Woke Up…My Mama Was Gone.
I Am Colored Pecola
The Sun And The Moon Are My Almond-Shaped Brown Eyes
My Full, Luscious, Pink Lips Speak Of My Mama's Wisdom
My High Cheekbones Form New Nations
My White Teeth Light The Pathway For Each New Generation Of…
I Am Pecolas To Come
My Nzinga Warrior Hair
Of Lamb's Wool, Curly, Wild, Kinky,
Nappy, Full of Static – Electric, Powerful, Glorious, And Mysterious Hair…

Spreads My Braids Across The Great Queen Continent!
My Hips And My Reconstructed Breasts
Decorate The Temple Of A Sacred Body!

Yes!
I Am Colored Pecola
I Am
Black
Brown
Cafe Mocha
Chocolata
Vanilla
And
Mulatto Spice.
I Am Colored Pecola
I Am
Beautiful!
I Am
Bold!
I Am
Bodacious!
I Am
Brilliant!
I Am
Bad!
And I Am Here
My Mama Was Right!

Hold Me While I Cry

Let me lay my head
Upon your breast
Embrace me
And taste my tears
Whether of sorrow or joy
Hold me while I cry
I am afraid to sleep
Make a safe place for me to hide, so I can rest
When my soul is weary
And I am waste
Ready to die
Cradle me in your arms
Keep me eternally safe
Hold me
Hold me
Hold me…
While I cry
And my soul shall be set free
Just hold me…Please!
Just hold me while I cry.

Will He Still Love Me Tomorrow?

He said I was like a snowflake…
I had my own distinctive twists and turns
I was not like any other woman whom he had ever met
And when he looked at me
I grew
My husband, he's a charmer
He would always reminisce about the first time he had seen me
It was a party, I was with my girlfriends
My hair was in a French twist
I had the perfect little black dress on
Size 10!
He said he noticed that I had perfectly round breasts
And legs like a dance.
"Are you a dancer?" he asked.
I laughed
"Sure," I responded with a wide, mischievous grin.
From that night to this, we have never been separated
And here we are, almost fifteen years later
Needless to say, I am no longer a size ten
But I still have great legs
And my once perfectly round breasts
Ahh, well, they have a story all their own.

Tonight…
Time and space

Hurt and pain
Confusion and distress
Pressure and uncertainty
And more bad news from the doctor
Has caused me to become
Frightened and secretive
My perfectly lovely round brown breasts
Aren't so perfect, lovely, or round anymore
And I can't help but wonder
Will he still love me tomorrow?
They said that I had to have the surgery!
The infamous "they"
It was no longer an option
Either I lose my life
Or my Sickly brown breast
I think that he took it harder than I did.
I had already conditioned my mind to the reality
That I might have to part with my breast
I had prayed and cried about it everyday
Since learning that I had 'IT.'
'IT'…meaning breast cancer!
Even the word CANCER sounds so dark and menacing!
Let me get back to my breast
It seems that a woman's breasts to some men are their mommies!
They cuddle all up underneath them
They are the focus of their affection
They serve as a woman's calling card
The size of your breasts somehow determines your sensuality
They are given names
They wear fancy bras like men have cars!

They are remembered on Valentine's Day…
It's called dresses me in fancy lingerie
My breasts my gals, my hanging-on-in-there pals!
Sagging or dragging, perky or a pimple
They give your figure shape and form
Confidence and attention
Given honorable mention
They are a sight to behold and often they are held and caressed, kissed, but soon they will be missed…
And I wonder if so…
Will he still love me tomorrow?
I remember the first time I felt something odd inside my lovely breast
It was a tingle, a pain.
I must confess I did not at that time have annual Mammograms
I kept putting it off
My girlfriends kept telling me that I was playing a dangerous game with my life.
I thought that they were just being dramatic!
But this irritating pain would not go away!
I went to the doctor and sure enough
She said that she could feel something.
She took my hand and taught me how to do a breast exam.
I had never done one on my own before
I guess I was afraid to touch…
Afraid to touch my own body.
I was taught that it was unnatural to touch yourself
I guess I took that a little too far!
Now…
How do I tell him that I have to see another specialist?

Will he understand?
Will he be supportive?
Has the cancer spread?
What does it all mean?
Will I be sick a long time?
Will I die?
What if I do lose one of my lovely brown breasts?
He has always said, "Nobody is cutting on my wife!"
Will we struggle over that?
Will he still love me…?
Whatever tomorrow brings…
In sickness and in health
Until death do we part?
Death really knows how to do you apart.

The following week…
It is cold in the doctor's office
I feel so lonely
So uncertain
So afraid
So confused
I wonder why this is happening to me.
I was not diligent enough.
Today I have to have the lump aspirated
And tomorrow the dreaded results.
A S P I R A T E D?
It's the same kind of word that the doctor used when my mother died.
We're sorry that your mother E X P I R E D at 8:30 am.
She expired like a date on a can of beans!
At 19 years old, I didn't understand that terminology and its relationship to my mother's life

What do you mean she expired?
She died?
I feel that same way today.
There is a chance that the lump could be cancerous.
Cancerous meaning that I could have a malignant tumor
I don't doubt my husband's love.
I doubt my loving myself anymore.
I had told only one person what I was going through
My husband didn't even know
My sisters, my daughter, my son didn't know
Only my closest friend knew what I was going through.
Isn't it strange how we tell our girlfriends things we
don't tell anyone else?
I'm not sure if that's good or bad.
It's just my reality right now.
My husband would ask too many questions that I
couldn't answer.
That would stress me out!
My sisters would simply make me feel guilty for not
having had a mammogram
And that would stress me out!
My daughter and son would worry and that would stress
me out!
But my girlfriend…
We have cried together through life's ups and downs.
When we got married, we cried
When she had a miscarriage, we cried
When she made me her daughter's godmother, we cried
When we gained and lost weight, we cried
When I got my first book published, we cried
We cried when we laughed so hard that we cried!
And when I found out today that the doctor found an

abnormality and that I
Positively had breast cancer and needed to have a
lumpectomy, we cried.
These are words I don't like because they aren't pretty...

        A B N O R M A L I T Y
          L U M P E C T O M Y
         L Y M P H   N O D E S
              RADIATION
             MATASTIZED
                TUMOR
             C A N C E R
           CHEOMTHERAPHY
          RE-CONSTRUCTION
             BE PATIENT!

Why did I have to see that needle!
Why! Why! Why!
It is a miracle that a needle can inject radiation into your body and
Newfangled machines can actually locate where the cancer is.
Many months later
Many sleepless nights
Many days of being tired
Many days of looking like a pitiful pariah
Many days on "chemo" and steroids
Many cold chemo conferences at the hospital
Many days of beautiful scarves and African head wraps
Falling off of my head
And feeling like a victim

Many nights of being held in my lover's arms
Many days finding sweet surprises under my pillow to cheer my days
Many afternoons getting forget-me-not flowers
Many Sunday mornings waking up to him praying over me
Many nights hearing him weep
Many daydreams of seeing my children grow up
Many more times to hear him say…

    Yes, I will still love you tomorrow!

Just Let Me Be Something
1972 for June

He said...
"If I could be the rain that falls against your brown skin...
Golden brown skin on a hot summer day...
I would cool you down and love you all around.
Just let me be something.
If I could be the moon, I would bathe you with my midnight glow
And kiss your cheeks
Kiss your cheeks
And give your hair a crown of twinkling stars
Just let me be something."
He said,
"If I could be the sand at Carmel, I would hold sea shells for you
Sea shells for you
I would whisper inside them your poems and my melodies of love songs.
Just let me be something."
He said, "If I could be a tapestry of fine linens with golden threads and beads of black pearls
Black pearls. I would wrap you up and carry you to the third heaven...
And there the angels would sing to you, Sing to you of my love

Just let me be something.
If I could be your smile, I would kiss your lips
If I could be your hands, I would touch your face
If I could be your arms, I would embrace you
If I could be your heart, I would beat in rhythms and rhymes
Just let me be something."
He said,
"I want to be something! I want to be something in your life...
The moments you treasure
The secrets you keep
The love you hold sacred
The prayers you pray
Something! Let me be something!
Just let me be something."
rip my love-2013
(repeat)

The Morning Is So Beautiful...
Love song for a friend

You said...
"The Morning Is So Beautiful
And I am thinking of you
While the dawn
And the dew...
Melt into warm, soft waves."
I said...
"When you feel me watching you
From time to time
Know that my eyes are full of love

For one so dear to God and me.
I want the best for you
That means space and time between us
You are one of the things
I cannot touch…too much."
You said…
"You are the wind for me, powerful and strong
Hushed, stilled, and unperceivable…
The morning bird cannot be separated from her song
Nor I thoughts of you…"
The Morning is so Beautiful.

I'm Still Here...Still Waiting

Good morning, my love...

I watched you while you slept last night.
You were so at peace. No worries, no troubles, no intruders.
I was standing guard over you, my wings covering you.
Did you know that you smile when you're sleeping?
If you only knew just how much I love you.
Wake up, wake up sleepy head. It is time to start a brand-new day.
I have great things in store for you today. There are people I want you to bless, prayers I want you to pray today.
You forgot to say good morning, my love. You used to whisper a prayer before driving off.
Oh well.
I am still here. I'll be waiting…
Oh, I forgot you're in a rush again today.
Let me just get out of your way.
I hope we get to talk later.
I love you…
Drive safely. There are many dangers seen and unseen. I will go before you.
Did you hear me? She's gone again.
But I will clear the path for her safe passage.

Good afternoon, my love...

You were in such a hurry this morning that you almost hit that little boy who was crossing the street.
I moved him out of the way for *his* sake.
At lunchtime why don't we take a walk in the park and enjoy this beautiful afternoon.
I put the flowers in full bloom for you. The birds are singing, the butterflies are trying to get your attention.
Oh well. No time to see me in all of my splendor.
No time to talk to me again, you say?

You haven't even called me today. I never even crossed your mind.
You have not even acknowledged the promotion that you got on your job.
You never stopped to thank me for the good report from your doctor.
Oh well, maybe tonight when you get home we can have quiet time together.
See you later.
Oh ...I guess she didn't know I was talking to her.

Good evening, my love...

Surely now you will have time for me.
Oh, your favorite shows are on at 7, 8, 9, 10, and midnight?
You fell asleep in the arms of the midnight talk show host
And his goodnight kiss is a curse word.
I just don't understand why you don't talk to me

anymore.
Don't you love me anymore?
Don't you feel me anymore?
Don't you hear me anymore?
Can't you feel me tugging at your heartstrings?
Have I ever left you or forsaken you?
Haven't I always been here for you?
When you were sick, I healed you
When your house was going into foreclosure, I opened my window and shut the mouths of the bank holders!
When the vandals spray painted all of the cars in the neighborhood, yours was made invisible!
When you had that flat tire on that dark road, I sent my servant, "Good Samaritan," to stop and fix it for you.
When the doctor told you they saw a lump on your breast, I turned the tears of sorrow into tears of joy!
When your son went astray and your daughter got pregnant, I brought them both back into the house of God
When you thought you couldn't make it another day, you cried for me to take your very life!
I reached in and lifted you out of many waters!
I moved through the demonic forces of the universe to save you!
I do all of these things and more
yet…
You never tell me how great I am anymore
You stopped dancing before me in the sanctuary.
But you dance before him in the club!!
You never say my name anymore
But you cast your pearls among the swine of bad boys!!!
But they will only leave a sour taste in your mouth
But I am sweeter than the honey on the honeycomb.

Yes! My daughters, you know who you are
You pay their rent with the money I blessed you with!
But you are still mine, bought with a price, paid for in full, with my blood.
I reach for you all day...my arms are outstretched
I am waiting for you to run into them and be safe.
But you don't take hold of me anymore.

You have taken hold of the world and its songs, its styles, and its worldly wiles.
You think engraving my name on your arm honors me, but my word should be engraved in your heart!
You wear nose rings, practice witchcraft and voodoo, read tarot cards and tea leaves.
My daughters, like a precious jewel in the snout of a pig...cast not your pearls among the swine!
Have I ever forsaken you?
I have *never* forsaken you!
Why have you not chosen me to love?
Many are called and few have been chosen
But I have chosen you.

Here I am still waiting...waiting for you
Here I am alone...lonely without you
Here I am longing for your love...I love you.
I sacrificed all for you!
I would not deny you the very best of everything
I remember when you used to gaze at me and smile...remember?
I was the rainbow you marvelled at
Remember when you stopped to notice the little things...like the sunset at the end of a summer's day?

Remember when it rained and you held your face up to the sky
And I kissed you with raindrops from heaven?
I have loved you before and since the beginning of time
I have loved you deeper, stronger, and longer into infinity and all eternity.
My "love is as strong as death, many waters cannot quench it neither can the floods drown it."
-(Song of Solomon 8:7, KJV).1

I have loved you before day or night.
Before mountains and streams, rivers and oceans
I have loved you before wind or rain, honey or bees, before flowers and trees
or colors in the spectrum
Before stars and galaxies, or constellations or asteroids in the universe exploding
Don't you know that you are my heart and soul, mind and strength?

Have you forgotten the melody that was in your heart?

I need time with you
I need you more than silver or gold, fortune or fame, my arms are aching to hold you
I am starving…hungry for your embrace!
I love you! I am jealous of all that you put before me
I want to anoint you and turn all of the generational curses into generational blessings
I want to kiss you with the fruit of my spirit.
I just want you to talk to me...Spend time with me.

I want to tell you secrets and reveal mysteries to you
I want to give you your heart's desire
I want you to read my love letters, for in them is life
I want you to give birth to the songs that I planted in your heart
But…but you have fallen asleep

Ahh! Goodnight, my love and…

When night turns into day I will say…
Good morning, my love, again
I am still here waiting…waiting
Waiting for you
But where… oh my love, where
Where
are
you?

Look At Me!

Look at me!
Look into my eyes, do you see me? Me!
Not your idea of who you think I am.
Can you see the soft sides of me?
Or do you believe only what you have heard about my rough edges?
Can you see my brilliance and due diligence?
My sassy pizzazz?
Do you see my razzamatazz? Or do you only recognize me by the color of my skin? Yes, the skin I'm in?
Does my reputation precede me?
Black is loud, vain, profane, creates disdain.
Black attacks, snaps back, and rhymes rap.
What about my footprint on history's story?
My forefathers were inventors, scientists, aviators, mathematicians, doctors, engineers, lawyers, artists, authors, musicians, architects...poets. They blazed the trail...
Then suffered and died without glory or fame.
America's history, 400 years of shame! Look on me and be renewed
I am your sister of a darker hue.
Look at me and experience the fragrance of gardenias and the taste of honey upon my tongue.
Once a slave,

Now a Queen with a crown of diamonds, rubies, and gold
See me…
And behold!

Me and My Fender Rhodes

The music in my memory brought me home again
It called me back to my mother's lullaby
And my sistas' songs
Memories embrace me like a newly composed lyric does
a melody
You see, I am home again.
As the sun begins to set in New England skies
Ahh! Yes, I am home again.
Met by the fragrance
Of my sistas' breath – breathing life back into me…
Fills my heart's empty spaces
Erases all the pain
Heartaches and disdain

This time I did not waver in coming home
This time I ran into the arms of home
And rested on the stoop of my childhood dreams
Images of my happiest days play hide and seek…me
Touch me, taste me, and love me.

I fell asleep on my mother's pillowed couch
Ahh! I knew then that I was home
So I dreamt that I was tap dancing with
My fingertips upon the keys of my Fender Rhodes

I was wearing a fine black tuxedo with tails

That stretched from my dream all the way up
To Copley Square, then around and down to
Boston Commons and finally there on Newbury Street
Sweet…
I strutted my stuff, tough, tall, talented
In my spit-shined sneakers and tails
I shouted, "Checkmate! Checkmate! Check me out!
King me, people, king me!
But know that I am the Queen!"

Oh! what a scene I made in my dream.
Before sunrise, my eyes opened in the dark
My face towards the ceiling and from my eyes
I projected images from my mind and they were playing my life
Back and forth, and forth and back on the ceiling

While my fingers danced upon the keys of my Fender Rhodes

I lie still upon my mother's new bed
Unpacking my mind like a suitcase filled with my sistas' gifts to me
I embrace them

Then slowly the LA fancy lady in me
Begins to thaw the cynicism from my tongue
It drips slowly upon the keys of my Fender Rhodes
And music springs forth like a mandate to me
You see…

Morning bursts forth with the sweet aroma of

My mother's voice calling to me
And my sistas echoing the same
It reminded me of why I had come home again

To gather broken pieces of myself…
To heal the haunting wounds of yesterday,
To release the pain, renew the passion, ignite the dream, relive the
Songs of my childhood days

To taste my own tears,
Face my worst fears
Ahh! I am home again…

No! I am whole again
My mother, my sistas and

Me and my Fender Rhodes.

Your Smile Throws Me

When I think of your face...
When I need a warm ember, I think of your face
I close my eyes and draw a picture of your smile
I think to myself
Your smile throws me
The way one side of your mouth lifts
When you smile
The way your moist lips part
When you smile
The way your teeth and tongue begin to show
Just a little, not a lot
When you smile
The way your cheeks rise when you embrace
Your smile
The way your dimples dance in laughter
When you smile
Did you know that your eyes twinkle and your nose turns up?
Your eyebrows wrinkle and your nostrils flare when you smile
When I think of your face
When I need something to remember, I think of your face
I close my eyes and draw a picture of your smile

And I think...
You smile that way only for me.

When I Look at Your Face

Your face in the morning
Oh! Baby
Your face is so beautiful
Your skin is so smooth
Smooth like the jazz dancing off the fingers, from Erroll Garner to John Legend
Your skin is as smooth as the voice of Will Downing singing…
"Bess, you is my woman now!"
Your face is perfection…love
Sculpted by divine intervention
Honey baby, you are flawless
When you speak, your cheeks dance up and down
And up and down upon your face
And your smile is like Broadway, New York, and "The Hit Parade"
Sunday's best got nothing on you!
Patent leather shoes and strawberry shortcake…my favorite
Your face is like "Digable Planets."
"Black like dat, cool like dat, black like dat, cool."
Mandingo warriors have nothing on you, my love
Your smile leaps off your face like
Songs leap off the lips like…Ella Fitzgerald scats!
Baby, your eyes are like two deep pools of spring water
I see my own image floating in them

Your eyes embrace me
Like the sun upon my skin

Every length
Width
Depth and
Breath of me is embraced by your eyes
Your eyes make me blush and bat my lashes
Your nostrils flare when you smile
And when you inhale,
You exhale cool vigor
And when you speak, your words are hot and spicy,
Juxtaposing rap and rage
My love, my love
Your lips are like…like…like
Nothing in the universe that I have ever seen, tasted, or felt!
The ring around Saturn has nothing on your lips
The morning dew on the magnolias have nothing on your lips
The honey that the bees make
Is not sweeter than the nectar from your lips
Morning breaking into a new day cannot
Compare to your lips.
You have the lips of a Malian prince
Your lips on mine make music love and happy, sassy, rhythms beat in time
and play in tune
Ooh!!!! Baby, that's your face in the morning
I can't wait until….

My Greatest Love

We were married. Two kids having a baby.
The only common bond of love…
You!
You are my water, water, my "mending wall,"
With every breath…I breathe you!
You are the universe and the galaxy
I love you, son.
You are cool like black satin
Smooth like jazz on a Friday night
The universe reverberates when you embrace me
You!
You are a long drive with the top down
A soft summer rain kissing my face
Yes, a mother can love a son like that!
You are heartache sometimes
My midnight blues…"worryin' bout cho."
You are deep conversations on the drive home
My fix-it man…
You have style, class, and finesse
Too cool for school
I love you…
Like David loved the Psalms
I watch your every move…pray for your every step
I look into your eyes and I see you…seeing me.

Oh, yes, I see you.

Inside out and outside in
I love you, son, like a sonnet loves Shakespeare
If a sonnet could love "O! that you were yourself: but, love you are."
You are my greatest love
And that's that!

I Will Come Home Again

I will come home again
I will come home again
while the sun rises in southern skies
where the wind carries
the fragrance of sweet magnolias
tantalizing my nostrils
yes, I will come home again
and rest on the stoop
of my childhood memories like...
dancing on my daddy's feet
I see the images of my happiest days
playing hide and go seek on the block
"Swing me higher, Daddy, higher!"
I will come home again
and not waver
but rush into the arms of home
where rest is waiting for my weary soul
where love's embrace melts the northern
chill from my heart
I will come home again
and my fingers will dance
upon your face and catch your tears
"Mommy is gone, Daddy,

Just us four and not one more."
nothing is as sweet as your tears

Oh! Yes, I will come home again
and my lips will taste your tears
and your smile is sweet joy to me
welcoming me into the arms of home
and now...
where you are is home.
"Kiss Mommy for me."
I will come home again

Vessel of Love

I tried defining love…
As though it needed meaning and I understood it!
I wonder…
Can I be more loving?
Someone told me
That I was a vessel of healing
A taste of sweet wine
A well spring of water
A mountain retreat and
A candle burning bright.
Am I no longer poetry?
A song to be sung,
A dance of rhythms,
A beating drum?
Am I no longer a lovely work of art, set holy and apart?
Have I fallen with wounded wings, am I flying in staccato beats,
a meaningless thing?
I tried to find love…
As though love were lost instead of me.
Why can't I make my chair be a safe place for loved ones to rest?
I wonder…

Is my home not filled with love, laughter, peace, and friendship?

I wonder
When all human influence is gone
Why my home does not echo who had been there
And who lives there still...
Or have I just willed it all away?
Someone told me that my bed
Was a peaceful place to sleep, and that my pillow
Was a safe place to weep;
That my arms were like the arms on my easy chair,
Reaching out to hold them there.
They said that my eyes were like
Two oceans...
Pools...
Beckoning...
Full and forever true...
Charms...
My eyes and my arms.

A Poet said to me...
"God called and she got in the boat and rowed.
The tide rose up and her spirit just overflowed.
Joy surrounded her, like five little fishes and
a few loaves of bread.
Sorrow receded as the cowry shells begged to
adorn her righteous head,
'Mama Che'... Mama Che'... Mama Che'."
Hear the call of God's ocean, and
rub it on you like lotion...
for there is a balm in Gilead."
And that's what the Brown Poet said.

Where is that woman of whom he speaks?
Where is she?
For a long time I couldn't see…
That the vessel of love
I was searching for…
was right here
inside
of
me.

My Dance

I must dance because I was born under the sky of adversity!
I was raised in the soil of pain.
I waded in the waters, launched out into the deep
I leaped into the mouths of sharks
My bones formed the railroad tracks in the ocean
No chains around my feet, no noose around my neck
I must dance because if I don't keep my feet moving
I will get caught in the undertow of society's hatred of…
The skin I'm in!
I cry out to the Lord, "Why do they hate me so?"
Surely not because my skin is black!
But because they are afraid of who I am and what I can become
I must dance or I will die.
My soul will shrivel up.
I dance for my life.
I dance to music, art, science, medicine, math, engineering, architecture, and technology!
I dance to the sound of the pen upon the paper and my fingers upon the keys
I dance when men curse me, chide me: admonish me, lambaste me, rebuke me,
scold me, upbraid me, berate me, reprove me, censure me, chastise me,
reprimand me, lecture me, take me to task, and haul me

over coals!
The hateful atmosphere I live in mandates that I must dance!
Dance over my enemies. Dance over their heads, stomp on their tails
and muzzle their slithering tongues. With what will I stop them, you ask? My Dance!

A Love Song for My Mama, Vonceil Evelyn

I Remember Mama

There was a television show on many years ago; it was in black and white. Maybe it was on in the late 50's. It was called "I Remember Mama." That's how I got my new name – remembering Mama.

I was 20 years old when my mama died. I was just leaving my terrible teens. "It was the best of times and the worst of times." A time when a young girl needed her mother one minute and couldn't stand her the next! Have you ever been there?

Mamas challenge you on every word and deed. You resent their intrusion into your private little world and you envy her and wonder why she takes up so much of your daddy's time. Some mothers and daughters even compete for his hugs and kisses. Oh yes! I remember Mama.

I was taken from my mama at birth. She had contracted tuberculosis. It was May 1947, the year I was born. She was taken to a sanatorium in Perrysburg, New York – the now permanently closed J. N. Adams Memorial Hospital. It was south of Buffalo, New York, where we were living. "We" meaning my daddy and two older sisters. I cried for my mama, but only my Daddy-mama came. When he could not comfort me, he sent me to my

Grandma-mama, who tried without success to comfort me. I was also sent to live for a spell with my Aunt Sista-mama in Mumford, Indiana. That's when my two fingers became my best friends. I couldn't keep them out of my mouth. One finger was for Mama and the other for my daddy.

My daddy sent me to Chapel Hill, North Carolina to live with a family friend because he had no one else to keep watch over me. She soon became Mrs. Aunt Rebecca Clark-mama.

Later, when my Daddy-mama was able to care for me, I moved back to Buffalo, New York, where my daddy hired a babysitter who became the Strange Neighbor-mama. I had not even turned five years old and I had five different mamas!

And all I wanted was My Mama.

I had two older sisters whom I didn't even know. They lived in Atlanta, Georgia with one of their godparents. It was a stable home environment. Why did I have to be the throwaway?

They used to tease me because I cried all the time. Oh! How my soul cried! And when I couldn't sleep, my two fingers comforted me.
I always cried myself to sleep saying...
"I want my mama." I couldn't keep from crying for
My mama,
My mama,

My mama,
My mama!
Oh yes! I remember Mama.
It was December 21, 1952. My mama was coming home "cured" of tuberculosis after five years! I was five years old and it was five days before Christmas.
We all drove to Perrysburg, New York in my daddy's big Packard car. When we arrived, it was about 8:30 pm. The other patients were crowded on the balconies, hanging out of the windows, all waving and yelling…
"Goodbye Vonnie and God's speed!"

The windows were decorated with red, green, and white Christmas lights. It was an awesome sight for my little eyes to behold. I thought, 'My mama must be special.'
Oh yes! I remember Mama.
I remember them singing, "I'm Dreaming of a White Christmas."

I was the baby, so I got to sit next to Mama in the car. I couldn't stop looking at her. When she smiled, her smile embraced me. I could smell her body, all creamy sweet and clean. I rubbed her soft skin against my small hands. I listened to her soft voice. I had forgotten how it sounded.

I wanted to reach up and kiss the inside of her dimples but I fell asleep in her arms and to the rhythm of her heart beating. She wrapped her arms around me on the long ride home. I was five years old.
Oh yes! I remember Mama.
"I'm Dreaming of a White Christmas"

It was a cold, snowy day on December 21, 1967. I was 20 years old. Mama was in the hospital for minor surgery. It was four days before Christmas. I was the first one home from college. Daddy and I had driven Mama to the hospital at 6:00 am. She had packed her red and gold satin bathrobe with her gold slippers. She smiled at me, much like the smile she had given me the first time I saw her face.

She said, "At least I'll be home for Christmas." For some strange reason, I felt uncertain.
Mama looked at me and said, "Sweetie, you must have a will to live. Remember, you must always have a will to live."
Oh yes! I remember Mama.
Mama went home December 21, 1967 at 8:30 am, four days before Christmas, in a cold, sterile hospital in Niagara Falls, New York.
Mama came home December 21, 1952 at 8:30 pm, four days before Christmas, from a cold, sterile hospital in Perrysburg, New York.

The doctor said,
"Your mother expired."
I said,
"What does 'expire' mean?"
He said,
"Your mother died."

I thought, 'Mama must have been special for God to have

taken her so soon.'
I guess she was right.
She said she'd be home for Christmas.
She was only 50 years old and gone too soon.
Daddy and I left the hospital with Mama's red and gold bathrobe and gold slippers.
I couldn't keep from crying like I used to do...
Mama...
Mama...
Mama...

Oh yes! I remember Mama...
The smell of her body, all sweet creamy clean
Her soft brown skin
Her loving voice
Her dimpled cheeks
Her soft, fine hair
I remember the songs she sang to Daddy
The early morning prayers before school
Her big brown eyes

We never had time to argue in our 20 years
I never grew impatient with her
She never got on my nerves or made me sick
I never resented Mama or wondered why she had all of Daddy's attention
I never considered her intruding into my life with good advice
She was only 50 years old!
Gone too soon!

She was Aunt Vonnie but My Mama. Her name was Vonceil.
It is my new name now...Che'Vonceil
I hope it will be the name my son gives his daughter.
It will be a name passed on in remembrance
her great-granddaughters
Alexis Vonceil
Ava Vonceil
Oh yes!
I remember Mama.

I Am a Thread
1974

I am a thread
And my life
The needle
That guides me
And weaves and knits
Me...

To my mother's womb
Full of pain bound in dark sorrows
And missed opportunities
Yet
She was a gentle spirit
A touch of silk ribbons
And perfumed
Kisses
My mother
Gone too soon
My mother's womb

I am a thread
Stitched to my father's heart
I pulled and tugged
Into tangled knots of tenderness
Squeezed between the threads...
Soft for me

But hard for my sisters
Something good went wrong
Inside my father's soul

I am a thread
Woven into my sister's…sister's dreams
Of golden staircases
Crystal glasses, shattered images, and
Traces of dried tears on satin pillows
And the fragrance of forgiveness on
My sister's…sister's cheek
My sister's…sister's dreams and ex.pec.ta.tions!

I am a thread
Knit into my husband's
Nightmares of responsibility
Can't give love you never got
My husband's back against the wall
I'm his nightmare, after all
Threads apart
Divorced by heart

I am a thread
Bound into my lover's wish
That I was white powered poison
Breezing…Speeding through his veins
I surrendered to my lover's wish

I am a thread on a spool
Woven into my son's life
He wears his father's coat of approval and disdain
And my love is an altar of prayers and a mantle

Of hope for his future
Of many sons and daughters to come

I am a thread
Who can comprehend?
I am a thread of many colors
I am sewn into the very fabric
Of all those I love and hold dear

I
Am
A
Thread
On

.

A
Spool
Spinning
Towards
The
Promises

I
Am
A
Continual
Thread

Love Song for Helen Keys

In Memory of Helen

My breasts.
Loving yourself is hard.
Especially when you've been told your entire life that you are fat!
Fat according to the standards set by society
Your nose is fat
Your lips are fat
Your face is fat
Your hips are fat
Your thighs are fat
Your stomach is fat
Your arms are fat
Your big toe is fat
Your butt is fat
Your breasts are fat!
"Whoop! There it is!"
My breasts.
The ones that were brown and round
Firm and lifted up when I was young
And then again, after the reduction
Radical, ain't it!
Now…
No one can mock my fat breasts.
They are gone.
How shall I describe thee…Cancer?
You are like white powered poison

I shall call you smack down!
You are a Stalker!
You watched me grow up
You followed me to the doctor
You saw my supple breasts
You lusted after them because…
They were firm
They stood at attention
They garnered too much praise.
You grew jealous and envious of…
My breasts.
They were healthy
I loved them.
They made my sweater fit just right
Every dress I wore adored them
My fine blouse buttoned up without a pucker because…
They were perfect.
Then you revealed yourself and your plan to…
Execute them!
You are a killer!
Your mission…
"To steal, kill, and destroy."
I remember your words, Helen
"Che' love your breasts! I don't have any."
Now your voice is silent.
My beautiful breasts.
I speak of you in poems, rhymes, songs
I speak now in an anaphora…
"For everything there is a season, and a time…
A time to be born,
A time to die,
A time to plant,

A time to pluck up what is planted."
A time to love...My breasts.

My Bed

Put love songs to sleep
A place of respite, solitude
Where I go to de-stress, let off steam
Quiet my mind, calm my nerves
Dream
My Bed
My first lover
Soft pillows dress her like a beautiful bosom does a plush woman
She is plump and warm
A lovely comforter like a fine dress drapes her wide king-size hips
Fine linens lay beneath her dress like a well-kept secret that only Victoria knows.
My Bed
I set the mood
Dimming the lights, lighting a candle
Soft music the prerequisite for our tryst
I shower
I pull her dress back, it falls at her feet, revealing…
Her fine linens, they are enticing and sensual
Her arms are open
She beckons me to come
Glass of wine in hand
I lay upon her and
Sigh at last…her fragrance, gardenias

My Bed
Her body soft and warm
Her linens crisp and clean
My body climbs across her lap
She embraces me
Her pillows cradle my head and with each toss and turn
she sings me a lullaby
I let myself go
I breathe in deeply and exhale. I fall asleep soundly, held
within her embrace
My Bed
When the sun rises I leave her with great reluctance
But I am refreshed, having been captivated by her
passion
In appreciation of
My Bed
I offer her my potion of rich vanilla and lavender oils
I tenderly massage these oils deep and hard across her
back and between
The crevices of her feet, all the way to the core
Hoping it will keep her wanting more…of me.

II

SONGS OF LIFE

Freedom is Coming Today!

I'm killing the dogs and clowns, snares and snakes and rats…in my life!
I'm weeding out the tares,
I'm cutting them to shreds,
Turning them to shards, setting them on fire.
I don't want to be touched by evil anymore or tainted by hands set to mischief
No more tongues wagging, whispered words of wickedness.
Freedom is coming today!
No more clowns to fool around with
No more merry-go-rounds…going nowhere but around!
No more weak-kneed jokers on bended knee asking for my hand
Thieves, railers, and revilers. It was I who left the key under the mat…ME!
No more stealers who stole
My dignity,
My crown,
My perfumed, sweet, melodious gardenias.
No more giveaways, no more trade-ins, just returns.

Freedom is coming today!
When freedom comes, I can dream again.
When freedom comes, I will have a renewed vision.
When freedom comes, anointing will be there with it.

When freedom comes, I will dance again, just like David danced!
When freedom comes, I will sing and scat like
Ella Fitzgerald, Sarah Vaughn, and Jill Scott.
When freedom comes, I can trust again.
When freedom comes, I can love who I am and love you for who you are.
When freedom comes, it mandates that I must…
Do
Be
See
Hear and dare others to be free just like me.
Freedom is coming today!

My Tribute Part I

I Am My Mother My Mother is Me

My Mother was the thread
And her life the needle
That guided me
And knitted me to…
To my mother's womb
Her pain our bond
Of dark sorrows
Inside of her a monster grew
Who knew
Her pain our bond
Of sweet joy
I am her legacy

I am my mother my mother is me
She will not see me cross the burning sands of time
Hold the scroll of graduation's reward
Or see me dressed in cap and gown
She will not share mother/daughter secrets anymore
Or smile at me from across the room
My mother will not wink at me when I have had a success

There will be no best wishes when I walk the flowered aisle

She will not see me dressed in silk and satin ivory white
or…
Wearing something old, something new, something borrowed…
I'll just BE blue and light a candle in remembrance of a life well lived.
There will be no more birthday cakes, lunch dates, or late-night phone advice
She will not be at my bedside when I give birth
But we will whisper her name in prayer always, in all ways.

I am a thread now
Tied to missed opportunities and unfinished conversations
Gifts partially wrapped
Questions I still need answered
And only a mother can hold you when loneliness has captured your memories
And holds them at bay

My daughter asks, "Where is Granny, Mommy?" I answer,
"I am my mother, my mother is me.
Look, she's right here inside of me."
When you look at me, it's really her you see.

Many moons have passed
And now…
My daughter is a thread…
Sewn into my mother's wishes and my dreams

Of her becoming all she sets her heart and mind to be.
We can't be silent.
Knowledge is power and that's the truth I see!
I am my mother child and my mother is me.

We are all a thread
Trying to break through generations of just not accepting
That cancer spreads
We are leaving a legacy for our daughters and their daughters' daughters
We must teach them to love their breasts enough to care
We must sing the song of life, the melody is…
In our voices
In our songs
In our dances
And in our poems
Love your breasts
Some of us don't have them anymore
Some have lost their voice

Today we have a choice
We cannot be silent anymore
There are just too many of us dying
For lack of knowledge
We are all threads
Composed of many colors
Grandmothers
Mothers
Sisters
Daughters
We are united because we are women
We are on spools of thread

Spinning and evolving
Uniting all things unto ourselves
Making a garment
Called life!
I am my mother my mother is me
You are me
And I am you
We are one
In this fight against breast cancer
It is a fight for LIFE!

My Tribute Part II

Silent No More
A Song of Sign for Aunt Grace Echols

Can you see my hands? They are my voice
We can no longer remain silent
There is a deafening sound in silence
A generation of women has come and gone
We must break the cycle of silence

We can no longer remain silent

There is a numbing feeling of isolation
Can you hear my voice?
Are you reading my hands and face?
There is someone in this place
Someone here right now who has a story, who is a breast cancer survivor
Maybe you have lost a mother, daughter, friend, or aunt…
Speak up for them, tell their story

You cannot remain silent anymore!

We need to hear your voice.
We'll cry with you, celebrate too!

That you are still here
You are not alone
We may not be able to prevent cancer
But we can start trying to reduce the risks
But we must talk about it
And then do something about it!
Walk for life, run for life, donate time for life, and give for life...

We can no longer remain silent

We need to lift our voices to educate all women, to encourage all women but especially women of color and our sisters within the deaf communities around the world that early detection and screening may help save the lives of the next generation of mothers and daughters.

We can no longer remain silent

We must dispel false rumors, potions, and myths
We must stamp out ignorance because...
What we don't know may indeed kill us!
We can no longer remain silent
My voice is in your hands
I am crying out loud, I want to tell somebody that...
I feel alone
I feel isolated
I feel angry
I feel numb
I feel half, not whole
I feel ashamed
I am afraid!

That's it...
Let your voice break free
Let it break down walls and barriers...

Cry out loud if you want to...
Tell us what you want us to know...

The many voices of breast cancer
Listen to the many voices of breast cancer...

Does anyone hear my cry?
Does anyone care that this is day four of my chemo?
Does anyone care that I have to wake up every six hours
to take Zofran?
Does anyone care that I am nauseous, nervous, and need
to be held?
Does anyone know who I am?
What my name is?
That I am 37 years old and have never had children?
Does anyone care that I have breast cancer for the second
time in seven years?

Does anyone care that I have one-and-a-half breasts?
Does anyone care that I have had reconstruction surgery
Because what little breast I had left...was lopsided?
Does anyone care that I walked around with
Strands of my dead hair inside my pocket after it fell out?
Does anyone care that my mother may outlive me?
Does anyone care that my mother died when I was seven
years old?
And now my daughter is seven...
Does anyone care that I don't like bad breast jokes? They

are not funny, cute, or humorous!
Take it from one who is newly diagnosed in both breasts
– yeah, bilateral
Mastectomy!

Does God know that I am mad at him?
Does God know that I trust him?
Does God know that I am conflicted and confused about
what I believe?
Does anyone care that I am glad to still be alive in the
land of the living?
And it has been prayer that has brought me over!

We can no longer remain silent

We must break through the sound barrier of ignorance
Forge the mountains of hope
Tread the healing waters of Jordan
We are all a part of God's divine purpose
Life...is a dance of many rhythms and movements
Today we celebrate the breaking of silence
Today we light a candle
Today we dance

Because we have broken the sound barrier
And we are silent no more!

My Tribute Part III

A Song for the Magnificent Thirteen
Eternal Flame

For the generations of mothers and daughters
Which we all represent on this holy ground
We light candles to symbolize
The lives of women everywhere
Past…present…and future…
We whisper their names…
Your light will never go out
We whisper your names

My grandmother Mattie Eugenia Echols – the first to succumb to breast cancer
My aunt Dorothy Jane Echols Morgan
My aunt Grace Echols, who was deaf
My cousin Marsha Echols, survivor
My cousin Judith Maureen Echols, survivor
My cousin Eugenia Echols, survivor
My cousin Belinda J. Echols-Heard, survivor
My dear sweet Marion Jordan Moultrie
My niece Sherri DyAnne Moultrie Greene, survivor
My sweet niece Alexis Vonceil, just placing her here
My dear friend Helen Keys
My dear friend Julie Brown King

My dear friend Patricia Graham Hinsley, survivor
I sing your song today
This is my tribute to you
You are eternal Flames
Forever burning bright.

A Song of Life for Aunt Grace Echols

I SO LA TION

How can you begin to understand this world of isolation that I now live in?
It was not my choice…breast cancer…it was not my choice.
My world has turned into a world of silence and secrets.
A world of pain and confusion
Why me?
Why did this have to happen to me!
I want to run away
I want to curl up inside and just die already!
I feel guilty for feeling…
Who can I tell?
Who will not pity me more than I pity myself?
Have you ever known silence?
It is an unimaginable sound.
Look at me.
Can you hear me screaming?
I see you all laughing and talking, but I can't hear your voices.
I see you pointing at me, your face seems frustrated because I am not responding.
I am not responding because I can't hear, or speak, or feel.
Am I dead already?

I am in
I SO LA TION

Who Am I

Who Am I?
Who Is My Father?
Where Is My Mother?

What Is My Name?
Selah, to praise and to lift up.
Starts Out So Sweet
How Can Unobtrusive, Loveliness
End Up So Bitter!
Gardenia
Named After A Flower
Whose Fragrance Slowly Fades
Whose Petals Turn Over Into

Disappointment
And Despair

Who Am I?
My Name Is Self-Hatred
Yeah, Call Me That!
'Cause Can't Nobody Love A Woman With No Breast
'Cause Ain't That Why My Daddy Left My Mama?
See How Confused One Can Get Merging Childhood

Rejection With Cancer!
It All Eats You Alive.

You Know What?
Every time I Reach Out For Love
It Smacks Me
Kicks Me
Denies Me
Rejects Me
Mocks Me And
Belittles Me!
Maybe I Should Reach In For Love And Not Out…
Who Am I?
Call Me Fear
Because I Am Afraid That God Doesn't Even Know
Who I Am!

Testing, Testing...1...2...3...Testing!

I was always complaining that my arm hurt.
I guess it didn't occur to me to connect my arm and my breast with the rest of my body.
I kept saying, "I'm just getting old, that's all."
My hair is thinning
My hips are enlarging
My skin is drying
My nails are chipping
And my menstrual cycle is skipping...
Hallelujah! That's all I cared about!
What's an ache or pain here and there?
I guess I acted like I didn't care!
until that fateful day...
I was telling my girlfriend that
I had had this pain for so long and in the same spot. It never went away.
I just wished that it would go away!
That sounds so stupid now when I think about it.
My sister scolded,
"Girl, you better stop wishing, hoping, planning, and dreaming and take care of your business!"
You had better run for your life if your breasts are swelling, have redness, are darkening, are changing in size or shape, or are secreting fluids, and especially if you have a lump or hard knot!
What was she talking about?

I guess I was avoiding the unavoidable!
I just could not believe that breast cancer could happen to me!
So I ask you out there, I can see you...
When was the last time, or should I say the first time, you had a mammogram?
I promise I won't look if you raise your hands.
I can't believe my ears...(I heard you raising your hands.)
Some of you have never had a mammogram!
"I just haven't had time," you say!
What?
"I haven't had the time to get to the doctor."
"Girlfriend, I'm 'gonna' hurt you."
Let's see...time is relative (you think)
You had time to go shopping at Neiman's. By the way, I love those shoes!
You had time to eat lunch at Legal Seafood! You had the Fisherman's Platter, I do believe!
You had time to fly to New York to see Hamilton the play. We had a blast, didn't we?
You had time to vacation in Playa Del Carmen, Mexico this past summer.
Girl, your tan was out of sight!
You didn't bring me anything back, by the way.
You had time to plan the annual church bazaar. All they had were trinkets.
You had time to take that Caribbean cruise to Turks and Caicos with your family.
You had time to fry chicken, make beds, go to Whole Foods way across town, get your manicure, pedicure, and facial, get to the cleaners, drive two miles out of your

way for the perfect cup of cappuccino!
You had time…but do you get my point?
If you don't get that lump checked out, you may not have a life; that is the hard, cold fact of life and that will bring pain to all of us who love you!
Have you ever given yourself a breast exam?
What is a breast test?
It is called a mammogram!
Look, when you get into the shower or when you are lying in bed before you go to sleep
Put a pillow under your right shoulder, use the three middle fingers
Just raise your arm over your head and in a circular motion from under your arm
Towards the tip of your breasts, just see if you feel anything that's abnormal.
That's it!
That's it?
Girl, your daughter is 20 years old, you should be modeling good health practices for her.
She needs to check herself monthly and every three years professionally.
If your sister is 40, she should go annually for an exam.
It could be a matter of life and death.

But I have always felt very strange about touching myself.
Have any of you ever felt like that?
There's a part of me that's afraid…what if I do find something or feel a lump?
It just doesn't feel natural to feel myself!
I can hardly stand it when my doctor does it!

Here's what I do know
Look, it is a well-established fact that heart disease kills
four times as many women as breast cancer!
I know that women who have a family history of cancer
can be at a much higher risk for breast cancer.

Among those risk factors is pre-menopausal breast cancer
in one's immediate family;
Early menarche;
First pregnancy at a late age, or no children;
A habit of drinking more than seven alcoholic drinks a
week;
Low levels of vitamin A from a diet poor in green leafy
vegetables and beta-carotene;
And high fat intake.
I know that there is also a fear with some women
resisting or discontinuing hormone therapy due to weight
gain and the FEAR of breast cancer.
What do you have to lose?
Well, a lot if you find a lump after it has metastasized!
All I'm saying to you is GET A MAMMOGRAM!
There are no needles involved.
It's a harmless machine.
You stand up.
You are clothed from the waist down,
The top is not overly exposed,
You and the medical technician are in the room,
You hold your breath for the x-ray,
There is no pain, only discomfort for half a second.
You wait a few minutes,
Get dressed and go home.
If something is detected

The technician may need to take more pictures. Do not panic!
Only the doctor can check effectively if they see some abnormality.
They will contact you if all is well or if they need to see you again.

Well, this is the big appointment day...It feels so cold in this waiting room.
These people look so strange, so sad!
They all have blank expressions on their faces.
Do they have breast cancer?
Have they received bad news?
Or are they just afraid like I am?
"Excuse me, I have a 10:30 am appointment."
"Take a seat and someone will call for you shortly."
Goodness! These magazines are all two years old!
Who wants to read about finances while waiting to have a mammogram!
Nobody speaks to you. They just walk by as though you are invisible.
When are they going to call my name?
My butt is just too big for this little chair!
Finally!
She said, "Change into this gown and take everything off from the waist down." Remove my necklace.
Wipe under my arms.
She asked if I thought I might be PREGNANT! HECK NO!
Unless it is another immaculate conception, I better not be!

Testing, testing...1, 2, 3 testing
Do you hear me?
I had to lift my lovely breasts, one at time, between two plastic plates
That pressed tightly against them and
Hold my breath as the technician took the x-ray.
First one breast and then the other.
It was a moment of discomfort.
That was it!
I had to wait for a few minutes while the radiologist checked the film.
I was a bit nervous during that brief wait.
But everything so far was okay, nothing unusual showed up.
I was told that my doctor would contact me if she had any concerns.
If you're out there and you hear me
Please don't wait
Take care of your body and your body will take care of you.
It is the ultimate act of self-love...
Here is the gift I offer you...
My sister, why are you trembling?
Don't be afraid
Come on...take my hand, walk with me
Please take it quickly before you change your mind
Do not hesitate, do not change your mind...
Today is the day to receive knowledge
When you receive knowledge
It will give you POWER!
TESTING...TESTING...1...2...3...TESTING
Do you hear me?

The Weary Round of Life

Here I am again
Me
Lost it seems
Once again
Going around in the same circle
As before
Yet I am lost
There is no left or right here
No up or down
No in or out
Only this circle of doubt and fear
Sometimes I see in myself a glimmer of hope
But it quickly fades
There is a center in the circle
Sometimes I see myself there standing
But I am always alone...ever by myself
I am pulled, it seems, by some invisible yet powerful force
Back to the winding of the circle...I go
Around and around and around
I never get dizzy. Isn't that strange?
I never get tired because I am accustomed to this ever
Spinning...weary round of life.

I'm Crossing Over

I'm Crossing Over To The Other Side Of Victory
I'm Treading Out A Pathway To Greatness
I'm Building A Bridge Over Low Self-Esteem, Hatred, And Degradation
I'm Going Through The Valley Of The Shadows Of Toxic Folks, Dream Killers, And Gainsayers
I'm Scaling Dangerous Mountain Terrain Treading On Doubt, Hesitation, And Fear
I'm Leaping On The Back Of "The Joy Of The Lord Is My Salvation"
And Crossing Over Into The Land Of Milk And Honey
And The Cattle On The Thousand Hills Are Owned By My Father
I'm Holding The Basket Of Overflow And Overtake Me Is Its Name
I'm Planting Trees In The Desert Where God Said A River Would Flow
I'm Living In Houses That God Said I Would Not Build And Owning Land That Was Left To Me As An Inheritance
I'm Stomping On The Serpent's Head, For God Said I Am The Head And Not The Tail
I'm Reaping A Good Harvest, For God Said I Would Reap If I Don't Faint
I Am In A Race, So Call Me Steadfast And Endurance Because God Said,

"The Race Is Not Given To The Swift Nor To The Strong But To Those Who Endure To The End."
I'm Clay On The Potter's Wheel And He Is Making Me...And...

I'm Denouncing,
Poverty,
Low Self-Esteem,
Promiscuity,
Drug Addiction
And Generational Curses!
I'm Rebuking Sickness,
Disease,
Cancer,
AIDS,
Mental Illness
I'm Calling Forth Salvation,
Deliverance,
Liberty,
Anointing,
Prophecy,
Jubilee,
Victory,
Wealth, And The Favor Of God!
I'm Crossing Over...
Moving Up,
Going Forth,
And Breaking Through..
I Am A Rocket Blaster
Designed By The Master!

On Wings

APRIL 1999

*THIS MORNING
I AWAKENED INSIDE MY DREAM
FACE KISSED WITH EARLY MORNING DEW*

*I WAS ON WINGS
REALLY FLYING,
'WIZZIN'
WHIRLING IN SPACE*

*HELD IN BALANCE, UPRIGHT, ARMS SPREAD EAGLE,
UPSIDE DOWN, ARMS SIDE STRAIGHT…*

*CAN YOU SEE IT?
I WAS EXCELLING
PROPELLING
DOWNSIDE UP,
SIDEWAYS
FLOATING ON MY BACK
THROUGH CLOUDS BURSTING!
HEAD FIRST
FEET LAST IT WAS A
GOOD MORNING BLAST!*

*I WAS ON WINGS,
SOARING, SPINNING, TWIRLING*

Che'Vonceil Echols, PhD

FLYING FAST,
WAS I DREAMING?
I WAS RAPTURED, CAUGHT UP
OUT OF BREATH
I OPENED MY EYES TO THE SKY...
THEN GOD WINKED
AT ME!

I Can't Believe This Man!

I Have Loved Him Ever Since High School
I Was 18 Then.
He Was My Dream From Afar
My Prince Charming And He Never Knew It
He Was My Hope For A Better Future
He Dressed Nice, Looked Nice, Talked Nice
I Could Only Imagine Because He Never Spoke To Me!
I Remember The First Time We Actually Met
For Me It Was Love And Never Looking Back!
I Can't Believe This Man!
He Told Me He Loved Me And I Believed Him!
So I Married Him And Had His Baby
Cooked His Food, Cleaned His House, And For Ten
Years And Six Months I Took His Abuse, His
Unfaithfulness, His Acid Tongue, Tearing What Little
Self-Esteem
I Had Into Tiny, Insignificant Pieces.
Well, I Was A Kid Then, Now I'm Thirty-Five Years
Old
How Dare He Tell Me I Am Less Than a Woman
Because I Have One Breast!
He Has Only One…Hush!
I Gave Him My Youth And All He Ever Did Was Abuse
My Love And Trust
He Lied
He Cheated
He Stole The Best Of Who I Am

Now I Know I Allowed Him To! Now I Need Him To Be There For Me!
And Where Is He?
I Can't Believe This Man!
He Must Be Crazy To Think
That I Am Going To Stand By And Just Let Him Belittle Me.
I Have Suffered Too Much!
I Almost Lost My Life!
Lost My Dignity!
Lost My Hair!
Lost MY BREAST!
I Know He Did Not Go There!
Let Me Tell You Something
If He Thinks He's Seen The Worst Side Of Me...I Don't Think So!
He Took My Affection But I Won't Allow Him
To Kill, Steal, Or Destroy Anything Else, Especially My Self-Esteem!
I Can't Believe This Man!
I've Waited All Of These Years For Him To Find Himself, To Change, To Grow Up, Become Responsible, To Be A Good Husband, A Devoted Father, A Provider And A Man Who Loves God.
My Knight In Shining Armor...Is My Nightmare!
I Need Someone To Hold Me And Embrace Me; To Lift Me Up!
What About Me?
What About What I Need?
What About What I Feel?
I Can't Believe This Man!
He Left!

Inside the House That Crack Built

A Song of Grace

Inside the house that crack built,
Held together by the stench of funky flesh
And dried blood,
Held together by old sexy sweat and
A generation of my Great-Grandma Mattie's tears.
Inside the house that crack built,
Dark, dingy, damp, smoky rooms, rats
Squeezing themselves between the slats of a broken
Plywood floor.
Roaches speeding on saliva highways
Filthy toilets crusted over with dried body waste.
Inside the house that crack built,
Filled with the smell of premature rigor mortis
Death, you know what I mean, it was a "living dead"
crime scene.
Where dreams are deferred and words of praise never
heard!
Only the voices of demons crying out, crawling into the
crevices of
A lumpy cranial core, my mind the door...
And crack my whore!
Inside the house that crack built,
Me running crazy wild in steely gray streets
Reeling to reefer high rhythms and cocaine beats

Dope dealers, the pied piper, the skin poppin' viper who
Will wait on your soul until it is ripened!
Crystal meth, rock, coc, and heroin
Are drugs of my choice
Every time I used…all the demons in hell rejoiced
Inside the house that crack built
Where genocide and homicide coincide
Somebody save me from this jail inside
Life ain't no crystal stair and that's no lie
I had to care because my soul was in there…
Inside the house that crack built!

Being Beautiful is a Suffering Way

Food is my enemy but I need it to survive
Yet it's killing me
It has changed the size of my thighs
The width of my waist and the image of my former self
Why do I keep wanting what is forbidden?
I keep trying to feed a hungry heart
I keep trying to break free from the inner me…I see
The more I try to become invisible, the bigger I get!
The pain makes me feel
And food makes me full
Food is my monster master, toxic, crazy-making friend!
It taunts me with its sensual aromas
And the colorful flavors that it adorns itself in
Sauces, jellies, frostings, spices, and gravies and its dressings
It is sautéed, congealed, simmered, puréed, flambéed, and grilled
It tempts me to taste and see, ah! That's good!
Food loves me and hates me
I look at these cellulite thighs
But I still eat cookies and pies with tears in my eyes!
You know what my biggest fear is?
That if I lose weight I still might not…Love my/me…you see
I hate what I love, yet I love what I hate.
Food is my lover. Food is my comforter. It is my false

sense of security provider
Gluttony is a sin but fat is the skin that I'm in.
Oh but…
I *want* to be beautiful again
When the doctor told me I needed to gain weight
He simply gave me a license, a mandate, a charge, a demand, a command!
"Eat, drink, and be merry…"
So here I am, 60 pounds later and 60 years older and he says…
"You need to lose weight if you plan to live!"
How dare he scare me!
Being beautiful is such a suffering way.

My Journey

For the past year as a poet/artist, I wrote one poem.
I did not journal…
I have books with empty pages and no words upon them.
I am sick inside because words are stuck inside trying to get free…
I have allowed the spirit of procrastination, the spirit of fear, the spirit of laziness;
The spirit of doubt to wrap me up with this invisible string.
Once I whimpered to be free but when the box top was opened
I just laid there and looked up. I did not reach out.
So this year, 2016, I must continue my journey upon the path of words.
I must write but more than write…
I must produce the work to be read beyond the box.
I wonder sometimes if words have been taken from me?
Has poetic rhythm left me without a beat?
I wonder…
Do I still have what it takes to write the poems? The only way I will find out is to begin the journey...
My staff is my pen and once the words are written, who will listen?
Who will hear the poems?
Who will ride with me the waves of their prophetic utterances?

I see myself standing before the crowd, preaching my poems
Oh yes! I am a minister, a minister over words.
I see your smirk doubting me...
It used to matter, your doubting me, but it is 2016...
Your doubt does not determine the gift that God has given to me.
And what I do with the gift is between the Master and me!
At 69 years old...
I will dance upon the mountains, like the Roe that prances upon the mountain of spices!
And you...
Doubt, procrastination, and fear
Will have no part in my victory!

Survivors Dissertation/ The Year of Jubilee

I Have Come To Sing My Song Today. Because Today Is Commencement Day. This Is The Day That The Lord Has Made. It Is Time To Rejoice And Be Glad In It! Today Is The Day Of Jubilee. Our Night Of Weeping Is Over, Our Morning Has Come!
It Is The Season Of Jubilee.
"To Every Thing There Is A Season And A Time To Every Purpose Under The Heaven."
A Time To Be Born, Oh Yes! This Is The Time To Give Birth!
A Time To Sow And To Reap! Church, This Is Reaping Time!
A Time To Kill The Flesh And A Time To Heal.
There Is A Time To Weep And To Laugh, A Time To Mourn And To Dance
This Is Boogaloo Time!
This Is The Time To Embrace Dreams And To Follow Purpose.
It Is A Time To Take Up The Helmet Of Salvation And Stand Upright For God.
It Is A Time To Put On The Shield Of Faith And War Like Warriors Do To Bring Down The Strongholds.
It Is A Time To Arm Ourselves With The Sword Of Victory. The Word Of God!

It Is A Time For Jubilation! A Time That Is Right On Time!
Isaiah Says "Awake, Awake Put On Thy Strength O Zion. Put On Your Beautiful Garments O Jerusalem The Holy City, Shake Yourselves From The Dust, Arise And Sit Down, Loose Yourselves From The Chains Around Your Neck!"

(Isaiah 52:1-2)2

Kingdom Of God Come, Thy Will Be Done!
The Feeble Will Be Made Strong. Those Who Are Fearful Will Fear No More! The Eyes Of The Spiritually Blind Will Be Opened, The Ears Of The Deaf Will Be Unstopped!
The Lame Are Going To Leap Like Gazelles, Those Who Can't Speak Will Sing!
For The Wilderness Of These Times, Ha! The Waters Will Break Out And There Will Be A Stream Of Living Waters In The Desert Of Our Times!
God Said, *"Behold, I Will Do A New Thing; Now It Shall Spring Forth."*
God Said, *"I Will Even Make A Way In The Wilderness, And Rivers In The Desert!"*

(Isaiah 43:19)3

Oh Yes! This Is The Day That God Has Chosen That We Should Arm Ourselves With The Weapons That The Devil Hates…So
Put On The Garment Of Praise.
"Praise Ye The Lord. Praise God In His Sanctuary: Praise Him In The Firmament Of His Power.

Praise Him For His Mighty Acts: Praise According To His Excellent Greatness."

(Psalm150:1-2)4

Blast Out! The Trumpet Sound!
Beat Out A Rhythm With The Tambourine,
Dancers Dance, And Cymbals Roar High And Low.
If You Have Breath, Use It Up For Praise, 'Cause This Is The Day Of Jubilee!! Because If You Don't Praise Him, The Rocks Are Gonna Cry Out, The Trees Are Going To Wave Their Hands In A Chorus Of Hallelujahs. The Wind Is Going To Whirl Itself Into A Whistle For God And The Mighty, Rushing Waters Are Going To Harmonize.

For God Is Great And Greatly To Be Praised!
We Have Come To A Great Choir Rehearsal Where Each Of Us Gets To Sing Our Song.
It Is Like The Song That The Children Of Israel Sang When They Went Through The Red Sea. Moses And The Children Of Israel Sang This Song...
"I Will Sing Unto The Lord, For He Hath Triumphed Gloriously: The Horse And Its Rider He Has Thrown Into The Sea! The Lord Is My Strength And Song And He Has Become My Salvation." (Exodus 15:1-2)5
My God, I'm Going To Exalt Him Just Like My Daddy Did! And Prepare A Place For Him To Inhabit!
The Lord Is A Man Of War. In Case You Didn't Know It...The Lord Is His Name. Moses Cried Out With Jubilee...
And I Say To My Enemy Was Covered Up And Sank To

The Bottom Of The Sea Like Lead! You Heard What I Said! God Did It With Just The Strength Of His Right Hand.
Broke The Devil Into A Multiplicity Of Pieces Because God Is A Multifarious Force!
It Doesn't Matter Today Who Sings Lead. God Hears All Of Our Voices Of One Accord.
It Doesn't Matter How Close You Sit To The Front. God Sees You When You Praise Him
It Doesn't Even Matter If You Sing Off Key Or Forget All Of The Words.
Just Worship The Lord In The Beauty Of Holiness.
Even The Desert Is Going To Rejoice, Roses Will Blossom In The Desert!
Tell Me That Ain't A Jubilee Moment.

"The Rose Will Blossom Abundantly." Isaiah Said That. And Then It Too Will Rejoice And Sing. This Is What Will Happen In The Year Of Jubilee!
The Lord Says,
"Awake, Awake, Put On Thy Strength, O Zion; Put On Your Beautiful Garments O Jerusalem." (Isaiah 52:2)6
Shake Yourselves From The Sameness of Dust Rising,
Shake Yourselves From The Grip Of Fear,
Shake Yourselves From Unforgiveness,
Shake Yourselves From The Lack Of Faith,
Shake Yourselves From Stinginess,
Shake Yourselves From All Impurities,
Shake Yourselves From Low Self-Esteem,
Shake Yourselves From Witchcraft,
Shake Yourselves From Backbiting And Perfunctory Behavior,

Shake Yourselves From Pretentious Praises,
Lasciviousness, And Bitterness!
This Is The Season Of Deliverance, The Day Of Jubilee!
We Must All Rise Up In Christ From The Sameness Of
The Dust Settling.
We Must Wake Up These Dry Bones And Grab Hold To
Jubilee
Each One Of Us...Is Pregnant With Possibility.
Because This Is The Year Of Jubilee!
A Survivor's Dissertation

Inside My Skin #1

It was 1965...
On a train I rode
A white child cried,
"Look, Mama, a black lady! Look, Mama, a black lady!"
I thought...
It's not black inside my skin
Thieves do not hide inside my skin later to steal
Nor are black secrets kept
Inside my skin
Black magic is not spirited
From within my skin
Death does not lurk here, dress here,
Nor black cats meow!
Anyhow...
I am a Queen
I am an African Queen
An aquamarine river dream
And poet.
It's not black inside my skin
And you know it!
Inside my skin
An emerald forest find no!
It's a jungle with water lilies floating in rhythm and in time
It's all inside my philosophical, historical, intelligent African mind.

Inside my skin and out again
The fragrance of gardenias
And the taste of honey upon my tongue
And upon my throne I sit…
Wearing a crown of diamonds, rubies, and gold
I am BAD!
Bodacious child!
And BOLD!
It's not black inside my skin
I am not a moonless night
Or a black Friday…day
The black plague or black hearted
Inside my skin magnificent…
Temples, palaces, and pyramids reside
Yes, I am black, white child
Black and bold with nothing to hide
Don't cry, don't fear
It was your forefathers
Who brought me here!
It's not black inside my skin
It's just the skin…God put me in!

I am the one

Does anyone know my name? Who I am?
I am the one.
I am an elder voice from the past
Speaking into the present to release the future
My name is suffering long
Don't take this story light
It is my health care plight
I am the voice of the one inoculated with the smallpox virus
I was the guinea pig they used to determine the viability of an experimental vaccine
I am the one.
Does anyone know my name?
Where I am from?
Who my father is? Where *is* my mother?
I am an elder voice from the 1800's
I suffered pain to determine that the anesthesia ether worked for all mankind
It was tested on me, you see!
I am the one.
The medical doctors of yesteryear
Had boiling water poured on my spinal column to discover whether this was an effective treatment for typhoid pneumonia
It was tested on me, you see!
I am the one.

Does anyone hear my voice?
I am still crying out!
The medical doctors
Placed me in an open oven pit to determine if certain medications enabled them to withstand excessive temperatures. It was tested on me, you see!
I am the one.
Does anyone care what happens to me?
European and American medical doctors used my dead body in cadaver research, as young medical students looked on.
My body was stolen from cemeteries in order to maintain their supply!
It was done to me, you see!
I am the one!
Does anyone care how I feel?
I was an African American-Siamese twin who was displayed at medical
conventions as a part of a "freak of nature" to entertain doctors;
It was done to me, you see!
I am the one!
I am the 1932 Tuskegee syphilis study, in which 400 African American men, all poor, all formerly uneducated, were misused and abused as an experiment, designed to determine the impact of untreated syphilis on our bodies!
Penicillin, the antibody, was withheld from 200 of us even long after the study proved it could cure us.
It was the longest medical experiment in withholding treatment from human beings in recorded history. It was done to me, you see.

I am the one!
Treatment is still being withheld from me!
I am still a voice that cries out from the wilderness.
My civil rights were ignored. I had no civil rights!
I felt isolated, demeaned, and humiliated, violated!
There is still despair in disparity
There is still lack of access to health care
The words "poor socioeconomic status" refer to me
There are still racial biases
Unethical practices
And differential treatment
Can you here today help change this sick system that supports the genocide of a race of people who were slaughtered so others could benefit from medicine that was experimented with on me? You see…
I am the one.
African Americans have suffered long and are subjected to second-class health care; the very bodies of our ancestors paved the way for us to have first-class health care…
How long do I have to wait to be treated like a human being?
There needs to be a…
Racial
Ethnic
Approach to community
Health
Has the system forgotten about me?
Has my voice been silenced by the deaf ears of society?
Have the hearts of those with the power grown cold?
Is there no more need for my body to be burned and bruised? Tested on, cut open, or poisoned? Do you hear

that sound? Is it me crying out to touch the consciousness in your soul or am I merely a pariah of society?
I am the one.
What will happen to me if everyone denies my existence?
Will I die because I could not get what every human being deserves?
Health care?
Or maybe you just don't have any more experimental drugs to test on me. Is that it?
I am not begging for food, although sometimes I am hungry
I am not begging for a place to live, although I may be homeless
I am not begging for clothes or shoes to wear
Even though I am cold, with worn-out shoes
I am not begging for money, even though a blessing would be counted to your tab
I live in unhealthy conditions
I am nutrient poor
I am abused by society
Ignored by the system
My neighborhood is saturated with rodents, crime, the stench of garbage and fear
I am plagued with
Heartburn
Arthritis
Glaucoma
Asthma
All major cancers
Infectious diseases
Mental illness
Morbidity from violence

Stress
Respiratory concerns
To name a few
And all I ask of you here today is to be concerned about my...
Hypertension
Diabetes
Cardiovascular disease
Can you defeat those three for me?
My ancestors paved the road with their lives...
They had no choice, no voice...but a cry
And you are telling me that I cannot reap any of the benefits?
Their lives are my inheritance to health care.
And you are telling me by your unwillingness to provide financial support
That I do not count and that my ancestors have died in vain
Let me tell you how I feel...
Have you forgotten that I was young once? I was Strong, healthy, Beautiful, and curvaceous? I had a muscular physique and ripped abs!
Yeah, I am the one!
You don't look at me and see the spirit of life that I have left to live.
I need your help...to live
Doctor
Nurse
Lawyer
Social worker
Counselor
Pastor

Outreach worker
Lawmaker
President!
Take note, I still vote!
I may forget my appointments and what time to take my medicine
I may forget how many pills to take and where my teeth are
I may forget where I put my pocketbook or wallet
I may misread the directions and
Ramble on and take up your precious time
Please don't forget me. Remember when you needed me? Now I am the one who needs you
I have aches and pains. My knees lock, my hands ache, my back hunches over and
I wonder if I am still desirable.
I want to live, love, dance, go to movies and dinners, have surprise parties

Be included in the decision making of my health care plan
I am getting older, my short- and long-term memory have traded places but…
I still remember and long to be embraced, to be held and, oh yes, kissed!
I cry myself to sleep remembering when loneliness was not my bed partner
I cannot enjoy the fruits of old age if I do not have good health care!
How can we justify celebrating until all human beings in these United States have health care that meets the basic needs of survival?

I am the one.
Rising up from victimization and discrimination
From medical mistreatment
From silent passivity
From sterile statistics
From inequalities, inequities, and disparities
I am the one.
Rising up from psychological, physical, and social degradation
From being America's economic, political, and medical pawn!
I am not the one.
Who will be sent out to peddle and to beg for what is rightfully mine, to have HEALTH CARE!
I am not the one.

Who will any longer stand in line for second-class medical care?
As long as I am alive, I will fight for the right to be alive and to be healthy
And if one life can't be saved, nobody wins!
There is no paradise in the paradigm
If the paradigm doesn't shift!
Our elder citizens have the right to lift their voices, and if they cannot, we who are able must be their advocates. There should be a mandate for health care professionals to see to it that our senior citizens are treated as citizens and not as aliens! Every human being has the right to receive…
First-class health care services, access to information, treatment, and medicine. They should have the right to hospitalization and counseling services, as well as

financial support and insurance. This is regardless of socioeconomic status, education, or inability to communicate those needs! Because they are the ones whose legacy we stand upon today! If we secure their right to health care, we secure that right for all people of all races and ages to come

I say to the African American senior citizens of these United States

You are the one

You are the one

Who deserves the best of medical care, for if it had not been for you and those of the Diaspora, many of the medical mysteries would have never been solved.

Your bodies were used as human experiments and for this I say…

You Are The One!

What If

What if I had held you closer?
Loved you deeper
Kissed you longer
Now that you have slipped away
Are you in the moonlight?
Are you the butterfly on the daffodil?
Or the sweet taste of honey on my fingertips?
What if I had spoken up?
Why did I remain silent?
What if I had cried out loud?
Instead I wept in silence.
I look for you
Are you the hunger pang in the empty stomach of a starving child?
Are you the shame in the shadow box called home for a runaway girl?
Are you in the eyes of the abused?
What if I had said yes instead of no?
Reached for you when you reached for me?
When you were in the deep places in the water…
I heard you cry out
"Help me!"
"Help me!"

I turned away…too busy then
Or was it fear?

What if I had stopped to…
To look at you
To feel you
To hear you
To touch you
Would you still be here?
Would you be fulfilling your dreams?
Making your mark in the universe?
What if you were still here?
You would have loved stronger
You would have loved deeper
You would have reached wider
You would have given more
Why did I let you slip away?
You are gone
And
I am
Searching
For the place
Where
You
Are
What if I find you?

III

SONGS OF LOSS

If I Should Die...I Love

I love a lot of things
The beautiful red sunset at
The bottom of the hill at Carmel-by-the-Sea
The velvet sand that nestles between my toes and under
my feet
At the beach on the Riviera Maya
I love that
I love the peanut brittle at Monterey Bay...
The kind my mama loved
The smell of fresh-baked bread on the streets of
Jerusalem
And Aunt Dorothy's homemade pound cake
Honey, let me tell you how
I love Aunt Dorothy's pound cake!
Just think about all the things that you love
I love
The fat brown bottoms of newborn babies,
Their tiny hands that hold on tight
And honey drool kisses
And tiny hands that hold on tight
I Love
Long walks along the San Francisco Bay.
And standing atop Masada singing my prayer
in sign language
I Love
Freshly brewed Carolina coffee

With the grounds at the bottom of the cup
Thank you, Aunt Rebecca Clark
I Love a lot of things
Jazz! Blues! Poetry and mood indigo
Etta James and Dakota Staton's…
"My Funny Valentine"
Oh yeah, I love your smile and the way your nose flares
Just think about that
I love a lot of things
The smell of gardenias in my hair and your arms
embracing me
Right there
I Love
Wading in the Jordan River
Sanctification
Gospel music
Climbing the steps at Mars Hill and
Placing my prayers between the crevices
At the Wailing Wall
Israel
I Love her
I Love
God
I Love
Cruising on the Nile River
I love, really love
April in Paris and the
Deep, long, wet kisses of raindrops in June, cool breezes
Honey,
Let me tell you how
I love deep, long, wet kisses in June, cool breezes
And you

I love
I love
The smell of gardenias in my hair and your arms
embracing me
Right there
I Love a lot of things

A Song for Alexis Vonceil

Our Diamond Dove

Alexis Vonceil Hayes
August 25, 1998-May 24, 2016

"God is our God forever and ever. He will be our guide even unto death."

-(Psalm 48:14)7

Paris, she wanted to go and see the City of Lights...
Grandma Sand was planning the trip.
Heaven, she is standing in the city lights now,
Our Diamond Dove lived a short life among us.
We watched her grow from shooting star to a Diamond Dove.
We watched her physical strength fade from time to time
But we felt her spiritual strength take hold of God.
Yes, our hearts are heavy today and they will be heavy for many tomorrows.
Our eyes overflow with tears but
We will embrace Alexis in our hearts today
And from this day forth, our reason to live forthrightly will be to see our Diamond Dove again.

Her song will sing us to sleep and her name will rest upon our lips in the morning.
Have you ever heard her sing?
Heaven has our Diamond Dove now.
She is embraced by the almighty Creator!

She is not dead.
Oh no...She is fast asleep in the arms of God.
She has gone from birth to everlasting life.
The body has gone back to the dust but her spirit is with the Lord
When she awakens, all her dreams will have come true.
She will own a mansion in the sky
She will walk on streets paved with gold...
She loved shiny things.
She will wear a crown made of rubies and pearls
And drink water from the fountain called everlasting life!

Alexis was an amazing daughter
A loving granddaughter
A sweet and sassy sister
An endearing niece
A fun, fantastic cousin
A loyal friend
The best friend to her best friend,
And a passionate follower of Christ.
Oh, you know she loved Jesus!
Alexis loved life!
From 12 to 17 years old
She was in a battle for her life
There was so much that she didn't get to do or see.
Like...
Another sunset, another rainbow
Feel the rain on her face
Just one more time at the beach with Daddy...
One more hug from Mommy.
She would want us to live our lives to the fullest.
She'll be watching us with God from heaven's window.

She'll be blowing us kisses from above
We will cry ourselves to sleep tonight
But remember
Alexis Vonceil will have…
No more suffering
No more pain
No more heartaches
No more disappointments
No more tears…
Just peace forevermore.
We must pay her love forward
We must love deeper,
We must love richer,
And we must love stronger.
We will see her again
Jasmine, LL be comforted in that
So fly away, Diamond Dove, fly away, fly away, fly away home.

I Don't Want to Die

It is a time of unrequited love
Some would wish to die
At eventide when the sun has finished rinsing
The world with its
Bold and brazen glare
I reached for love
You held it back
It was at winter solstice
I felt the chill of…
Unrequited love

You ask why I have wedged my prayers to be loved
Between the crevices of the Wailing Wall in Jerusalem…
I answer,
"It is David's city, the cradle of God.
Surely, I can find love in Jerusalem
Amidst the bombing and the blood."

Unrequited love lives in the hearts of mankind.
Like Elijah under the Juniper Tree cried out!
"Lord, it is enough! Take away my life…I want to die!"

But I don't want to die
I want to live and with one long, deep breath of life…
Exhale who I am and why I was here
I hear the sound of my heart

Beating against the prison of my chest.

So what do I do now, now that morning has come?
I must continue on this path designed by God
Bow down to those who love me and pray for my recovery and my remission.

I must not waver in faith
But stand still in the holy stream of healing
Like the shadows in the sand that disappear
At eventide
I wait for love
I wait for embrace
I wait for healing
I wait even for death
I cannot die
Lord, take this bitter cup from me
But if I should die…
Remember me to my Father

Goodnight, Granny Echols

Goodnight, Granny Echols, your light will never go out
It will shine with an eternal flame
Always reminding me of a life well lived and full of grace.
I will remember your smile, your laughter, and your voice
I will remember the touch of your warm embrace.
God gave you to me for a time and now longs for your return
Granny, my love...you never gave up
I will remember your strength
You never stopped believing
I will remember your faith
You always sacrificed
I will remember your spirit of giving.
I will miss your voice encouraging me to
Press harder, climb higher, dream bigger
And keep forging against the raging waves of doubt
Good-bye
You have gone home, you are at peace.
You are resting safe in the arms of the Master.

"Good night, my husband
Good night to my eight sons and daughters
Good night, my great and grandchildren."

You have gone the last mile of the way. You have run the race;
You have kept the faith. "Well done, my good and faithful servant."
Goodnight, Granny Echols. We will see you again on the other side.

"Weeping may endure for a night, but joy cometh in the morning."

-(Psalm:30:58)

Ghost

For all the loves that left
Healing said just wait
But the pain became too great!
I only wanted you to hold me
See me!
Be me for a moment
Own it!
Tell me you care
But the feeling wasn't there.
Your love became a shadow
I became a ghost
You loved me less
I loved you most.

The Bear

For the silent ones
(i)

The Bear has ridden off into the sunset, it is unable to comprehend the rape of me.
The Bear is not able to take ownership of its grizzly behavior.
I let my guard down and in one moment in time,
In one thousandth of a second,
I was stolen,
Ravaged,
Beaten down and
Restrained.
Raped!
Raped.
Ripped away from all feelings and emotions.
Raped.
Physically annihilated and spiritually desecrated.
Raped.
Psychologically penetrated and mentally fractured.
Raped.
Broken and disturbed
Lopsided
Forever wounded
Intellectually twisted
Wounded forever

The bear
Took the best part of me.
I hate you.
When I look at myself in the mirror…I hate you too!
I see broken pieces, fragments/a distorted image
Shards of my former self.
Behind my eyes I held this secret
In my heart I cradled a heavy burden.
The secret that led me...
to the window,
to the balcony,
to the pill bottle,
to the needle
to the Cross.
I carried it alone, or so I thought
The secret was a sore on my soul
A perpetual throbbing pain
It whispered, "You are dead! The Bear and I raped you."
But I am silent no more.
No more secrets.

IT
(ii)

I don't hate You!
If I choose to hate
I stop the healing.
Hating you makes me remember...
I want to forget
I want to forget the way your eyes looked at me...
Yes, looked at me the first time you saw me as...
Your victim.
Hating you makes me seek revenge against something I can't control
Vengeance belongs to God!
Hating you keeps me from loving myself
Hate aims to kill my spirit
Hate weakens the source of my power
Hate seals in the pain
Hate refuses to allow love back inside of me
Hate makes me bitter and fills me up with loathing
Hate grips forgiveness and keeps me bound!
Hate makes me feel dead and alive
You know what I mean?
Hate...
You act as if you don't even know why

I should hate you.
It is out of my hands now...You know what I mean?

The Secret

i

I hold a secret deep and dark
I keep it hidden in my heart
And every now and then…
I think of him.
I get a twitch of pain
It digs and pinches me…
Keeps me in self-disdain

ii

The thoughts of him…
Whirl around inside my mind
Like a rope that squeezes tight…
While I'm sleeping…the rope
Comes creeping and scares
Me in the night

iii

It taunts me, mocks me
Then with laughter, loud and haughty
Keeps threatening me, reminding me
Of when I acted naughty
He said it was my fault.

iv
I was a child and he was grown
I trusted like a lamb
And through my life I was told…
If you tell, you will be damned!

v
And so I kept the secret
Like a special gift I treasured.
Then God revealed to me this truth…
That he loves this little girl called me
Beyond what I could measure.

IV

SONG OF SURVIVAL

You Are Not Forgotten

I pray that you will see the divine purpose for which you have been called.
You have not been forgotten
For you are that woman whom God took out of man
And breathed into her greatness
You must believe in your divinity?
You must believe in your Ecclesiastical power?
You must believe that you have power with God and influence with man?
You are that woman who stood at the well
You were accused and humiliated in public
You are that woman whom other women scorned…
As you drank from the heavenly father's everlasting cup
You are that woman who risked her life and said,
"If I perish, let me perish I'm going to see the king" -(Esther 4:16)9
Your name is…I am not forgotten
You stand tall in the lineage of Jesus
You are that woman who
Believed that there would be a
"performance of those things that were told to her by the Lord!" -(Luke 1:45)10
You are fueled by a million, billion, and trillion God-given sparks of light
You are a holy flame
Not of the world but in it just the same

A rocket blaster
Designed by the Master!
You are not forgotten
Today you find yourself standing on the precipice
Of an unfolding image of who you really are!
You are finally coming out of the darkness and into the light.
You can sing your song because nobody else knows the lyrics but you.
You have
"Run through a troop; and by my God have I leaped over a wall." -(Psalms 18:29)11
And now you can run like the roe upon the mountain of spices.
You are filled
With the spirit from on high
Come and spin like a circle of fiery flames.
Keep pressing against the darkness
Keep pressing against low self-esteem
Keep pressing against shame, guilt, and unworthiness
And you will break through the break forth...
And give birth to the king in you!
For you have been bought with a price
Redeemed through the blood of the Lamb!
You are the daughter of the Great I AM!
You have not been forgotten!
Never could be
You are that woman who was an outcast and cast out
You were a scapegoat
Mocked, laughed at
Gossiped about, lied about, hurt, wounded,

Counted out, never told the truth about
Always second choice
But now you have a voice
You are not forgotten!
Remember the little mustard seed
That grew into a mighty tree?
Remember the little boy
With his little fish and five loaves of bread
When shared fed many?
Remember the little cruse of oil and little meal
That the poor widow had for just herself and her son?
Well, it fed the prophet full
And overflowed when she was done!
Remember the little pots
That were filled with water at the wedding feast
That Jesus turned to wine so sweet?
Remember
"Suffer little children
to come unto me, and forbid them not:
*For of such is the kingdom of God." -(Luke 18:16)*12
Remember the little sheep that went astray?
And the little sparrow that God watches every day?
You are like that
Remember the
Little verse that *said, "Jesus wept."-(John 11:35)*13
That kind of love covers a multitude of
Sisters like you and me
You see,
Today I have come to give you a charge!
A mandate!
Start singing your song before it's too late!

"Nothing holds you captive that you don't romance."
Unlock the door, take off the mask,
In this life we have one chance, so...
Dance, dance, dance, and sing a song for your hair!

About the Author

CheVonceil Echols is a prolific writer who has been creating spoken word art for over 40 years. She has a master's degree in Counselor Education from Northeastern University in Boston and a PhD in Christian Counseling from Royal Priesthood Academy in San Antonio, Texas.

CheVonceil writes with power, profundity, and poignancy.

She has had the honor of reading for the former Poet Laureate of the United States, Robert Pinsky, as part of the Favorite Poem Project in 1999 in Boston.

CheVonceil has been called an anointed minister of words. Her poetry is prophetic, thought provoking, and revelatory.

She is also a performing artist whose stage presence has been described as majestic, mesmerizing, and inspirational.

Songs for My Hair is a book dedicated to 13 women in her life who have been touched by the multifarious forces of cancer. Each narrative is written from a real-life perspective, experience, and conversation.

Excerpts of *Songs for My Hair* have been presented in four stage productions – two productions in Boston and two productions in San Antonio, where she now resides.

Dr. Echols is a retired 30-year veteran teacher who has served as a family therapist, children's advocate, and Christian counselor, and who is dedicated to the ministry of service.

She is a devoted mother, mother-in-love, and grandmother.

Bibliography

All Scripture quotations are taken from:

The New Scofield Reference Bible Authorized King James Version,

Editor C.I. Scofield, D.D.

Copyright 1967 by Oxford University Press, Inc.

Copyright 1909, 1917; copyright renewed 1937, 1945 by Oxford University Press, Inc.

Annotations 1-13

Made in the USA
San Bernardino, CA
10 June 2019